Things Have Changed with Mummy, Daddy and Me

by Nina Nile

Mummy and Daddy used to argue all the time

And now Daddy doesn't live here anymore

I still live here with mummy in our old house

And I visit Daddy all the time in his new house

some days I am sad because things are different now

Other days I am happy because of all the new adventures we are having

so even though things

have changed

I still have mummy

And I still have Daddy

First Published in 2017 by Nina Nile Publishing.

www.ninanile.com

isbn: 978-0-9957063-2-3

Text and illustrations copyright © Nina Nile Publishing 2017. All rights reserved.

No part of this book may be reproduced or transmitted in any form without written consent from the publisher.

www.ingramcontent.com/pod-product-compliance
Lightning Source LLC
Chambersburg PA
CBHW041235040426
42444CB00002B/167